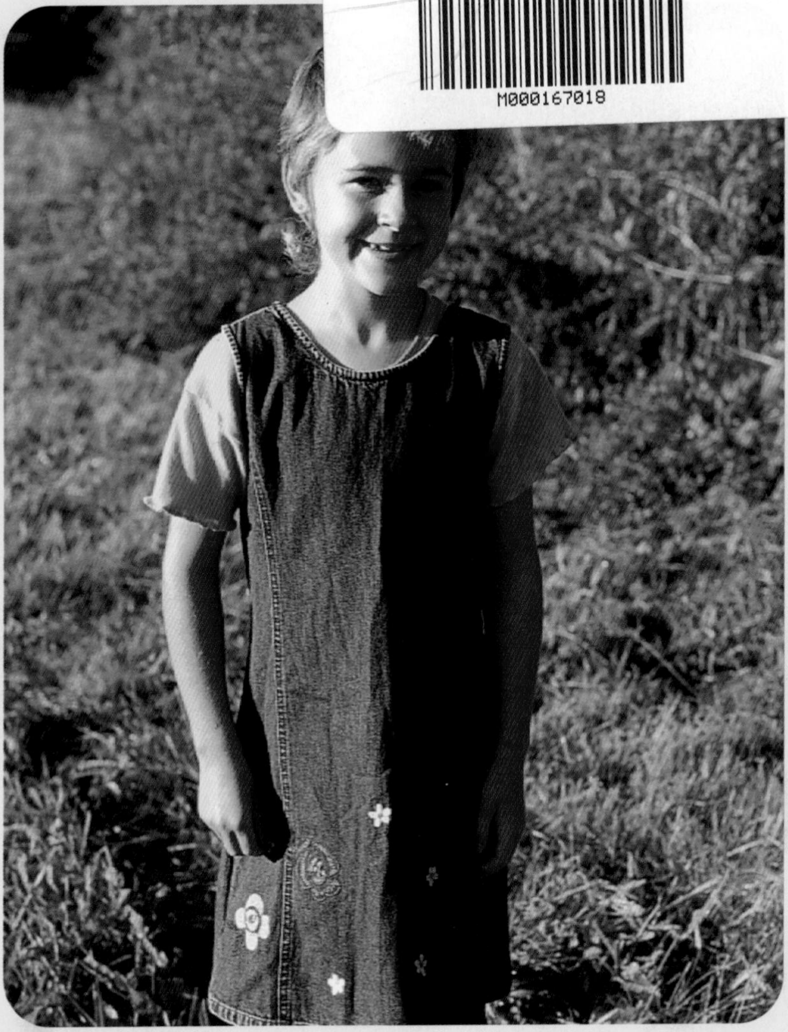

This is me.

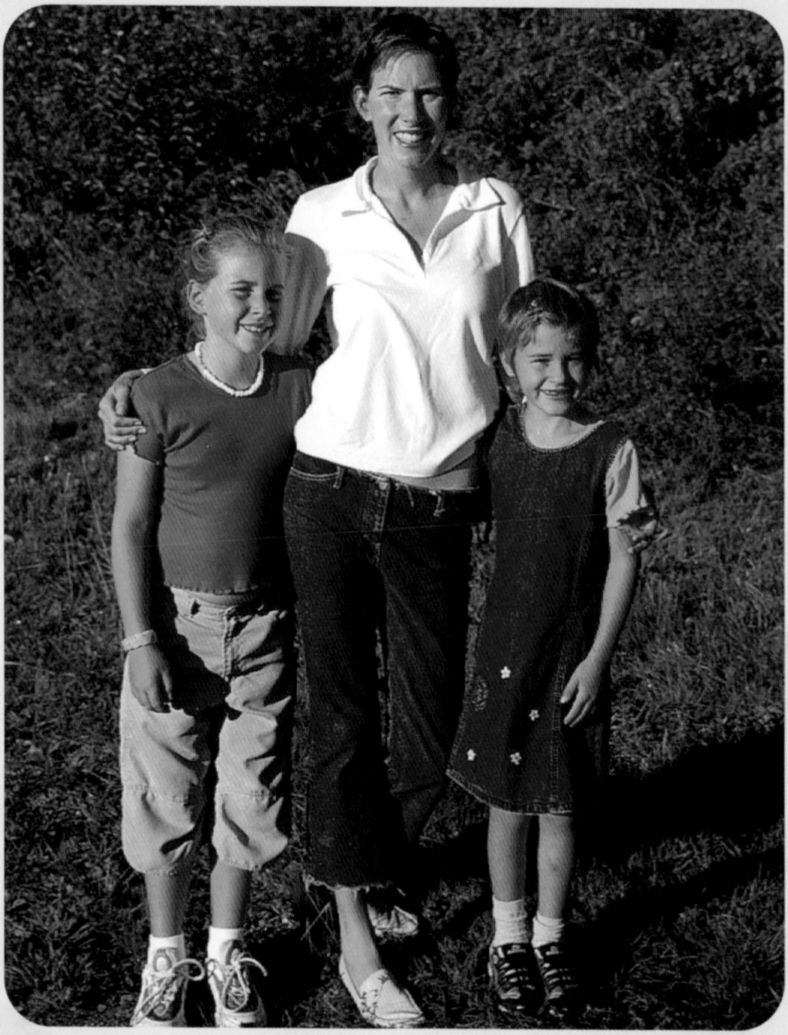

This is my family.

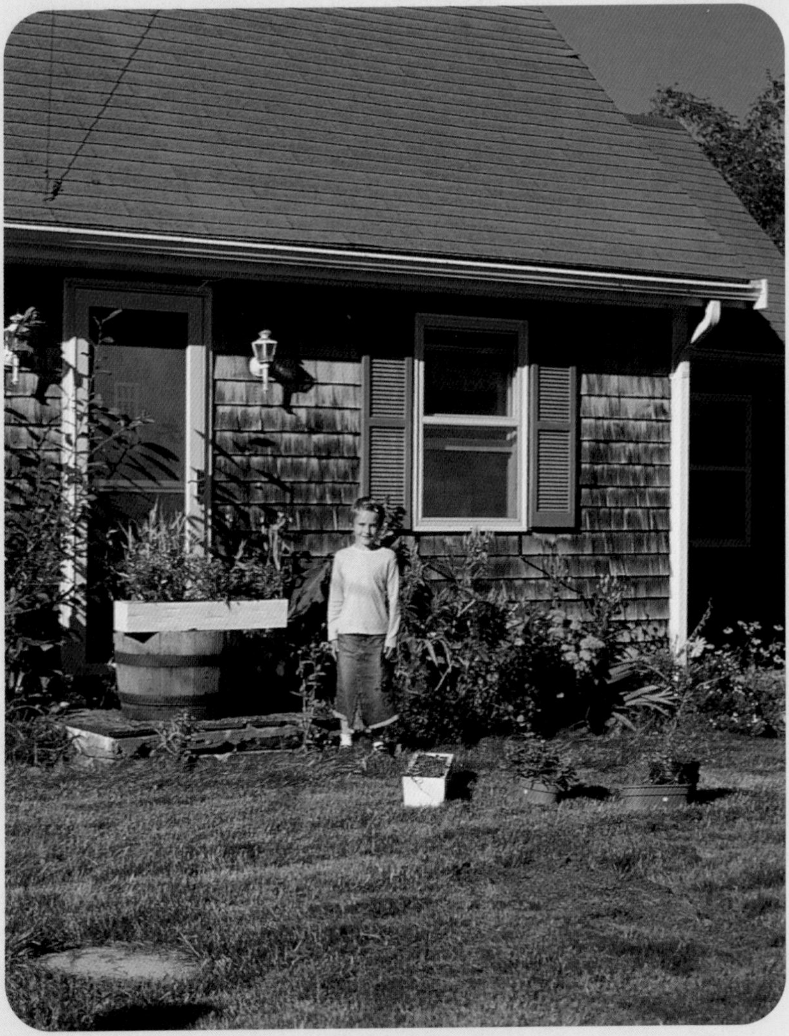

This is my home.

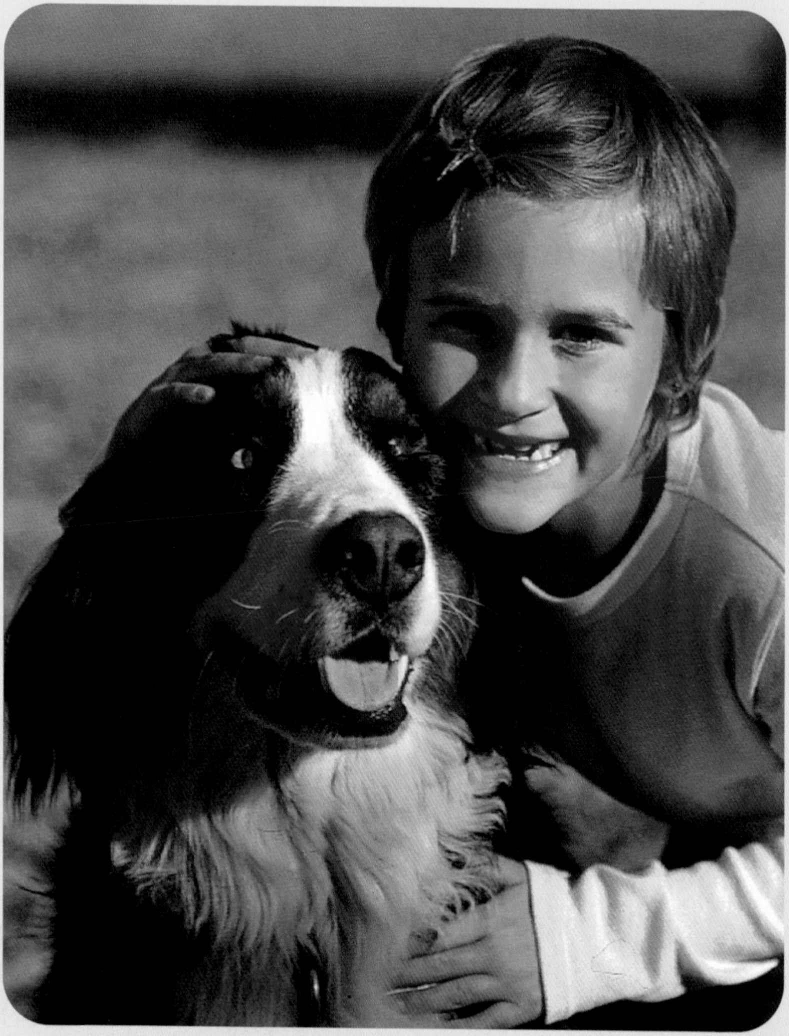

This is my dog.

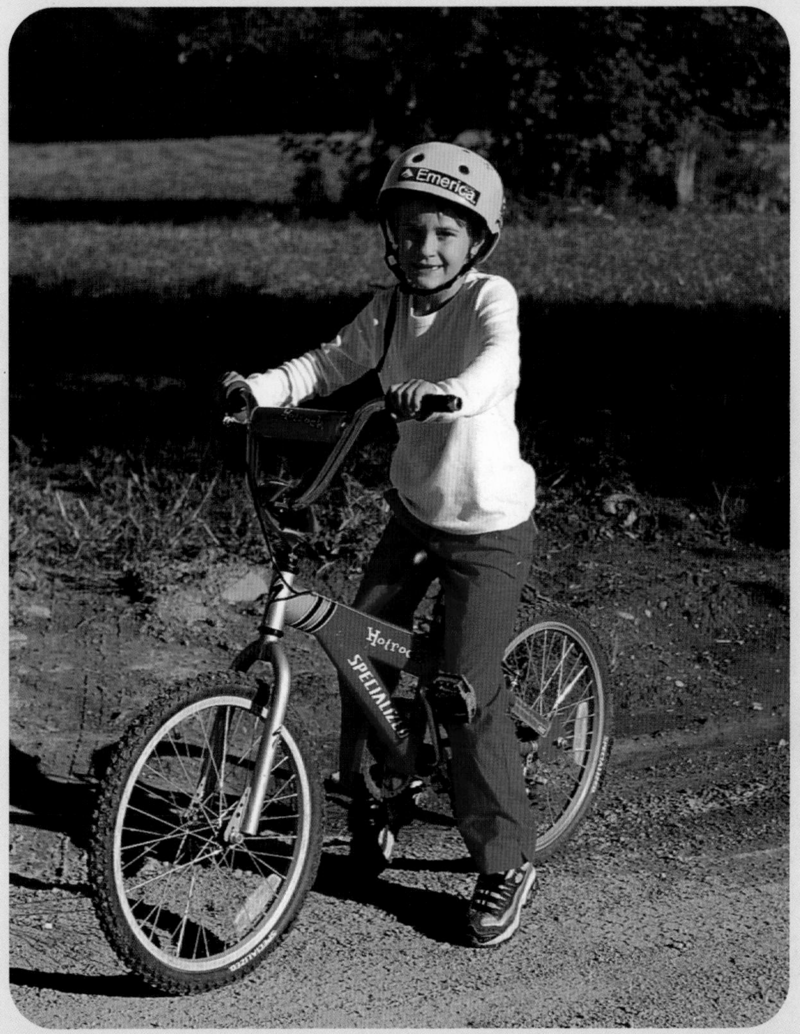

This is my bike.

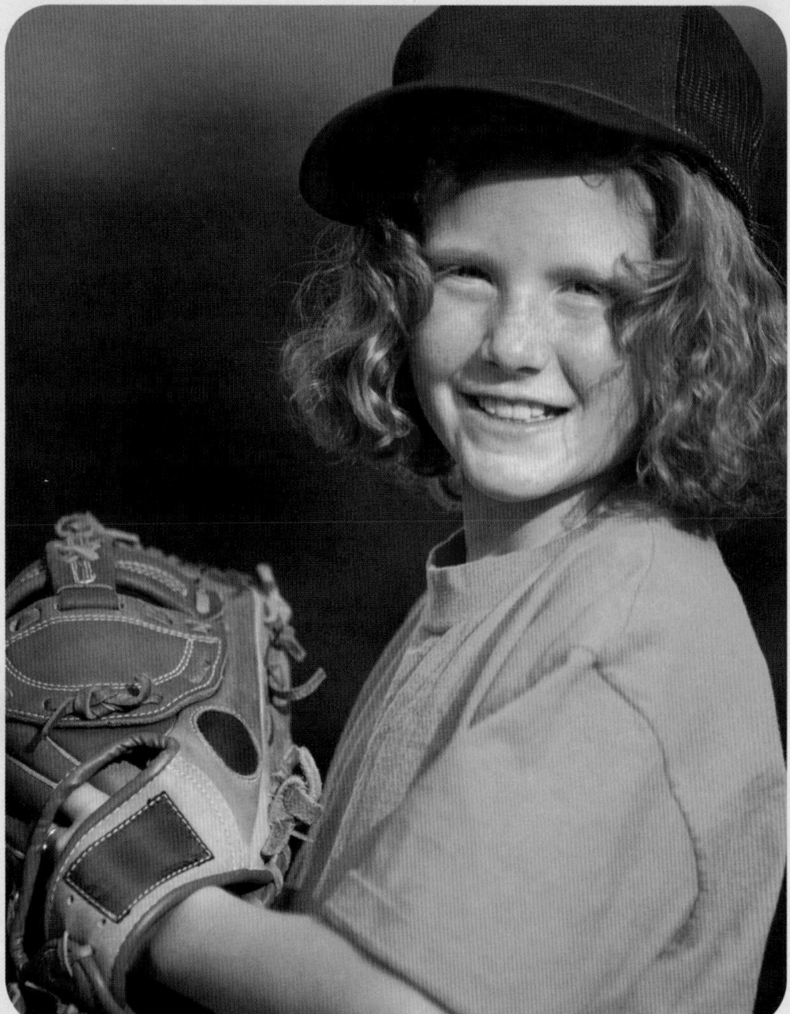

This is my friend.

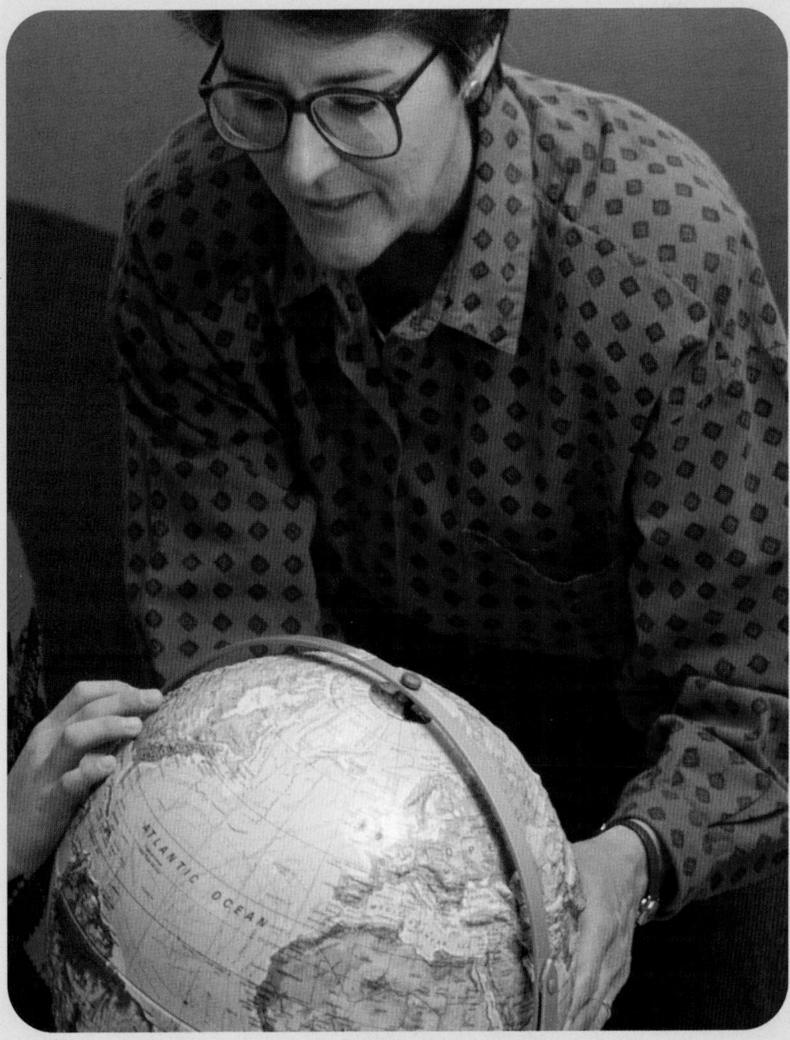

This is my teacher.

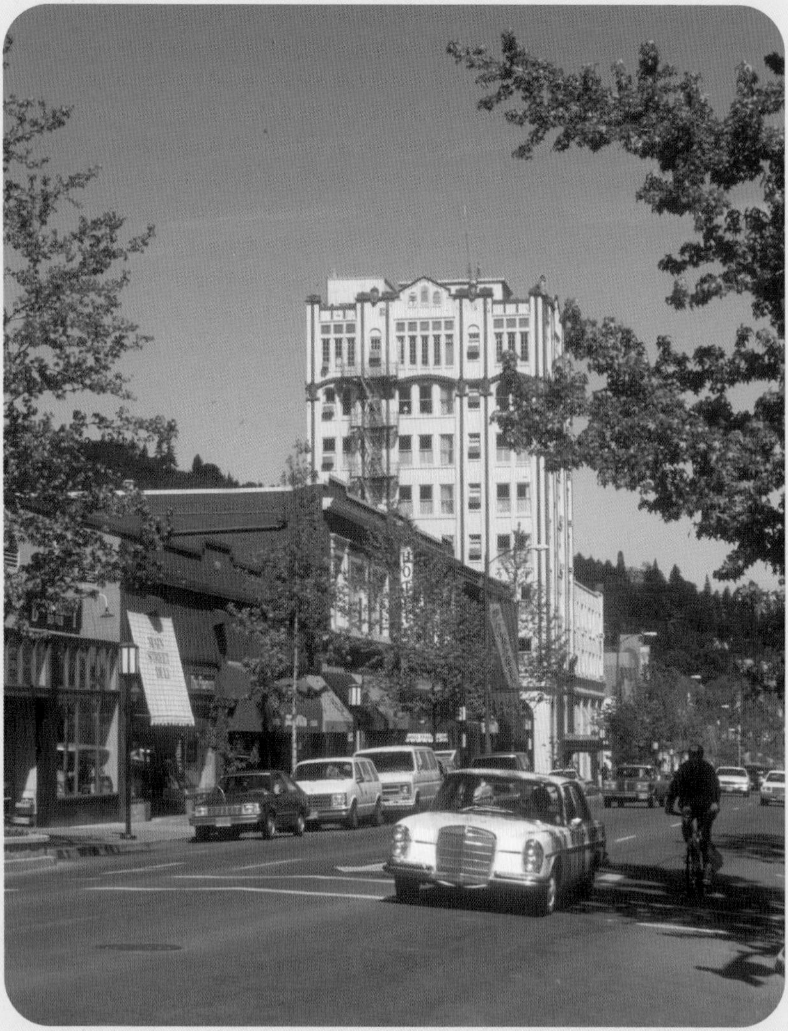

This is my town.